MESSAGES
To The True Descendants

Mu Skher Aakhu

Scribed by
Dr. Ra Heter

Universal Consciousness Publications

Imprint Universal Consciousness Publications

Copyright 2021

Published in 2021 by
Nuvo Development, Inc.
Decatur, GA 30034
404-549-4725

ISBN 978-0-9968000-2-0

Contents

Message from the Scribe
Introduction
Scenario 1 A Divine Being of Light 1
Scenario 2 The Shadow 4
Scenario 3 The Voice 8

Messages

1. The Shadow Explained 11
2. The Voice Explained 16
3. Words Are Alive 20
4. The Moment 25
5. Bending Space and Time 27
6. Defying Gravity 31
7. Crushed by a Rock 36
8. Once You Know Then You Know 39
9. What Dreams Are 42
10. Genie Out of the Bottle 49
11. It is in the Numbers 55
12. We Are in the Dark 58

13. The Curve	63
14. The Crappy Ones	67
15. Sitting in the Bathroom	71
16. You Are Not Going to Heaven	74
17. My Boys	76
18. The Fourth Grade	78
19. The Report Card	81
20. Dying Elders	92
21. Beyond the Light	97
22. Spirit Mail	100
23. Meeting in the Garden	105
24. A Body in Motion	111
25. Under Your Feet	113
26. Man is Perfect	115
27. Spirit Data	118
28. The Balance	124
29. Do You and Let Me Do Me	126
30. Diamond Doorways	128
31. Unified Heartbeats	131
32. Stacking Signs	134

Message from the Scribe

When I first met Mu Skher (*aka Timothy Spear*), I knew there was something special about him. As we continued to get to know each other (and eventually married), he would talk about his experiences and the difficulty he was having telling anyone because he didn't think they would understand.

Since I was reading a lot about African, Eastern, New Age, and other spirituality, I explained that indigenous people have been practicing what he was experiencing for thousands of years as mediums, healers, diviners, priests, shamans, etc., before they were told that something was wrong with it. Like many of us, he is just not in an environment that nurtures such a gift.

We began taking energy healing and other spiritual classes together, and one of the communities gave us our spiritual names. When I stumbled upon a reading that described Aakhu as a divine being of light, it became clear why Tim was given the name Mu Skher Aakhu.

Messages to the True Descendants

After years of having some interesting experiences with him, he finally agreed to be in conversation with me, and allow me to put into writing some of the messages that were coming through him. We have compiled some of these conversations into this volume, *Messages to the True Descendants*.

It begins with three experiences that shaped Mu Skher's awareness of interdimensional realms, and the rest of the volume consists of messages which came through him to deliver to you.

Ra Heter, MBA., Ph.D.
(*aka Dr. Patricia Dixon*)

Introduction

We are living in some very difficult and challenging times. This is because we have forgotten some fundamental truths about the multidimensional nature of reality, our purpose for being on Earth, and how to be in the world in a healthy and wholesome way that protects us and our planet.

How do we live in the world in a way that protects us and the planet? The true descendants knew how. *Messages to the True Descendants* is a book of inspirational messages that implores us to take an ancient, but new way of thinking and approach to reality. It is a book of messages that brings awareness to who you are, and how to lives as a multidimensional being in this multidimensional universe.

This book contains messages about how to use the powers that you come with, how to defy gravity, bend space and time, manifest the genious within, and more. It tells you how living life based good moral judgement and character protects you in this life and the afterlife. It includes messages about how to navigate through space and time so that you can carry out your purpose and the power you have to manifest what you want if you listen to the voice within.

Finally, if we all are to survive and thrive, *Messages to the True Descendants* reminds us that it is necessary to carry out our purpose and manifest what we want in unity with others, the planet, and the universe.

If you have found this book, these messages are for you.

Scenario 1

A Divine Being of Light

My family was facing a crisis, and my mother had to leave us in a childcare center at a convent with nuns for about three or four days. When this happened, I was about three years old.

The night my mother left us, when I realized she wasn't coming back, I was inconsolable. Because I would not stop crying, the nuns put me in a room to separate me from the other children, hoping that I would settle down. I was left in the middle of a dark room in a playpen by myself.

The room was dark, but the doorway was slightly cracked with light coming in. I stood there holding on to the playpen rails, staring at the door, just crying and crying, hoping someone would come in, but nobody came.

As I was standing there crying, the crack of the wall where the walls connected in the back of the room began to light up. It caught my attention because I thought someone was coming into the room from the back. I was waiting for someone to come through the door I was staring at, but I saw a light coming from the back of the room. When I turned to that light, it lit up the corner.

As it got larger and brighter, I saw the most luminous beautiful image with a smile and a vibration that seemed like limitless love, peace, and joy. She said to me, "Don't worry, don't worry. Don't worry. She'll be back." The presence that revealed itself to me was luminous, transparent, and had wings. It looked like clouds from the sky; like it used clouds from the sky to house its energy. And she said, "Don't worry, we'll always be here. I will always be here." Then she disappeared. I just smiled; she made me smile. I felt calm, at peace, comforted, and I was in awe.

As soon as she left, my brother opened the door and walked in. He reached up and held the rails on my playpen. I was standing up, looking down on him because I was taller as the legs on the playpen raised it about six inches off the floor. He looked up at me and said, "Timmy, Timmy, don't worry. It's gonna be okay. Momma's gonna be back. Don't worry, don't worry, stop crying, it's gonna be okay." By this time, I had stopped crying, but my face was still full of tears. I said, "Okay," and sat back in my playpen. Then he walked out of the room.

I have looked for that divine being of light since that day and I see her all the time. She comes when I need to be comforted, when I need information, and when I need direction. She gives me a glimpse of her presence through people to let me know I'm talking to the right person and that I'm at the right place at the right time.

I have looked for her ever since I first saw her. Because she let me know of their presence, I always look for them, and I see them all the time.

Scenario 2

The Shadow

My brother Leon and I would leave home and go to the transit station in Boston to go downtown to shine shoes. We were so young and innocent, I didn't even know that we had to pay to get on the train. And we were so small that we could walk under the turnstiles, the counter that you pay to get on the train; therefore, no one paid any attention to us. So, we would walk under the turnstile, get on the train, and go downtown to the Combat Zone, the red-light district to shine shoes.

Boston harbor is where all the ships come in for maintenance before they go out to sea. The sailors would be furloughed, and they would go into Boston, to the Combat Zone where all entertainment was; the movies, bars, clubs, and the girls.

Messages to the True Descendants

They wore black leather shoes which they had to keep shined. When they'd get off the ship and go downtown, we would be there with our shoeshine box. There would be many people from all demographics of the country and from all over the world. So we'd be there to shine their shoes.

The sailors would be with a girl and see us. Because we were so young, they thought we were cute The girl would say, "Ooooh, look at these cute little boys. Wow!" They wanted to give us money, so they would let us shine their shoes. Even though we were four and six years old, we could pop those shoes. They would say, "I want to show you those cute kids who can pop those shoes." And we were good at it because we knew how to spit-shine.

My uncle taught us how to spit-shine. This is the hook that nobody else had. When you are just about done, you get close, spit on the shoe, and pop that toe; you only do that on the toe. You spit on the shoe and do that last pop on the toe, and it is sparkly and shiny.

The sailors would be like, "Yeah!" And the girls would be like, "Ooooh," because it was a show. It cost about 10 cents, but they would give us 50 cents, 75 cents, and some would even give us a dollar. That was a lot of money because we're talking about 1962, and we were kids. They would give 50 cents, 75 cents, and a dollar to Leon and me. However, I was the one who made all the money. Because I was so small, they thought I was cute.

There would be groups of them who would come in waves. When we would shine shoes for a group, they would go into the theater, and our job was done. We would pack up and go home; we didn't wait for the next group. We would just shine the shoes for one wave, and then we would pack our stuff up and put our money in the shoeshine box, and leave.

One day, after we finished and walked around the corner, some 12 to 15-year-old boys were there, and they said, "Take their stuff, let's take their money!" They would watch us, and they were jealous of us. It was just Leon and me, tiny little dudes. And they said, "Take their money!" Leon kept a screwdriver he sharpened as his weapon. He put his hand in the shoeshine box to grab the screwdriver.

All of a sudden, an enormous shadow came over us. A shadow about 12 to 13 feet tall said, "Leave those boys alone!" All those boys took off!

They ran like they saw a ghost! And Leon and I went on our way to the train station.

When we got home, we gave the money to our mother. She returned the money to us, and we went to the corner store and bought some beans, bread, and milk.

Because we were doing good to help our family, from that day forward, I knew that if you do good, you will be protected.

Scenario 3

The Voice

At age 40, while undergoing surgery from a car accident, I crossed over. I had what is described by some as a near-death experience (NDE). I went from being unconscious to conscious; from being asleep to awake. I began moving up through space at an incredibly high level of speed and it felt like there was no gravity, no pressure, no air—nothing. I was moving so fast, it felt like I was standing still.

As I continued to go up, it seemed as if I was in a sphere looking out of a window crossing through rays of light. And there was something beside me. I couldn't see it, but I knew something was beside me because it held on to me, and I had no fear. It was like the elevator in the old days with the operator, who asked, "What floor?" and he stood beside you. He made sure you got to the exact floor and stopped it right at that level so that you would not trip over the threshold. That was how good they were. So I knew I had something beside me.

I went through a tunnel but never really left out of the tunnel area. The place I was brought to was the most beautiful, powerful light of all lights. It was so illustrious, so pure, so peaceful, so balanced that you knew it had the power to subdue, control, and create everything that's a part of our existence.

So I was brought to this place by the escort. You always have an escort that comes down and escorts you up. It represented me because the light was so bright that I could not look up. All I could do was bow. Behind the light was a voice. I do not know what it looked like because I could not look up. I didn't say anything; I just bowed.

The voice said, "Okay, I'm going to send you back."

Another representative that was there said eagerly, "I would like to go! I would like to go! I volunteer to go!"

The voice responded, "Well, are you sure?"

The representative said, "Yes! Yes! Let me go!"

And the voice said, "Okay," and we came back down.

But before we left to come back down, the voice said, "All you have to do is listen to the voice." We began the journey back.

When I came back, I recognized that the one that volunteered to come back with me was the one that had been with me all along. It was the voice that I heard through all that I experienced. It was the voice that I followed.

However, before this experience, I heard the voice from a distance. Now I hear the voice very clearly because it is right beside me.

1

The Shadow Explained

Your shadow is a dark space. Because it's a copy of you, you don't recognize that it is independent in and of itself. You are blinded to the reality that it is an entryway into another realm in the dark. It is just the dark that comes to the light that shows you its presence. However, since you don't understand that it is independent within itself and because it's a carbon copy of you, it allows your mind to remain at peace.

I saw a video of a two-year-old child running from her shadow, and she kept running from it. Children are pure and cannot say in words what they are seeing, what they are feeling, and what they know. She couldn't even talk yet, so she couldn't express what she saw or knew because she was still in the spirit world. She was more in the spirit world than she was in this world. She knew that there was a real presence behind her before she became integrated with this reality.

The integration of certain realities with this reality is how this reality keeps moving. Since you stay at peace, you keep it moving, but you don't know that your shadow is alive. Your shadow is there to protect you and keep you safe.

When you don't see it, it's inside talking to you. When you do see it, it's outside walking with you. If you were to see the reality of your shadow, it would mess you up. There are rules of engagement set up so they can't break the rules.

I am not clear. Would you explain further because from what we understand, the shadow comes from an object that blocks the sun or the light.

When the sun is out, we know there is darkness because when the sun sets, it's dark. However, darkness exists, whether the sun is out or not. It is another realm of existence, whether the sun is up or down. When the sun is up on this side of the planet, the sun is down on the other side. That is the polarity, sunshine on that end, darkness on this end, but it's all around us. When your body blocks out the sun, it reveals the darkness. It's with you at that time because it exists with things that live in the dark. So your shadow is one of those things that block out the sun or reveal the dark side of your existence when exposed to the sun. The sun helps us because if we stay in the dark, there's too much going on that our bodies cannot handle.

We wouldn't even be alive because the sun is the source of light that gives us life.

Our bodies are designed for the light and the dark, the day and the night. In the night, we shut down, and the dark does its thing. When the body is in motion, darkness is dormant in our lives, but it's not gone; it's still there. So we're living in the dark and with the light simultaneously. In the dark, the shadow side of you has its own life; it exists because the darkness is walking with you, even with the sun.

Okay, I am still trying to understand; I want to make this clear. So, we're talking about this as if the human shadow is something other than a physical phenomenon. There are physical objects around us. Every object casts a shadow; everything casts a shadow when the light hits it. But it doesn't have an existence in another realm; it is just a shadow.

The dark is with us 24 hours a day, seven days a week. If you allow yourself to be absorbed into the reality that your shadow is only the non-existence of light, that it is light that is being blocked by you, then you'll be limited in your understanding, realities, and abilities. Because human beings are living, they have a different relationship and connection with the darkness.

Okay, so you are saying because we are human beings, we have a different connection with darkness? Because we are alive, we have a different kind of relationship with it?

Yes. The shadow of an object is different from the shadow of a human being because the human being has a different connection with the dark. The dark space is another realm. It's another reality. It is a space that is occupied by many of a variety of sorts. When the sun goes down, your shadow goes back into the dark and blends in with the night. You just can't see it anymore, but it is still there.

Messages to the True Descendants

The darkness is where there is no time, and space is vast and unlimited.

Your shadow exists in that space and is there to protect you and keep you safe.

2

The Voice Explained

When we come to earth, we come with assistants to help us along the way. It is a birthright. When you know this, you know that you are not your situation or circumstances. You are not your economic status, your educational status, where you live, the house you live in, or the car you drive. You are none of these things. However, if you know who you are and the assistants you have to serve you, all these things can be achieved.

When you say we have assistants, what do you mean?

I'm talking about those who walk with you. Those you can call on to help you. They are servants that you have at your disposal to help you on your journey. You have been taught to fear them. But they are not your enemy. They are not ghosts or monsters. They are there to serve you. If you do not accept them, if you continue to deny them, you will continue to be powerless against your situation or circumstances. But if you open the door and unlock them, they will do what they have been doing all along; they will serve you. You just don't know that it's them.

So you are saying we have these servants. How do we connect with them?

All you have to do is know that they are there, and then they will do the work. All you have to do is accept them and stop running. Stop running and face whatever it is that you need to face. If you're faced with a situation, take a deep breath, have a conversation, listen, and you'll get the answer. You must come outside of yourself. You must stop running, challenging, and fighting. And you'll get all the answers you need.

Sometimes when you are faced with a situation, you hear different voices. One voice is telling you one thing, while another voice is telling you something else. How does a person know which one to listen to?

All you have to do is have a conversation. If it is not coming back right, then you know that's not the voice to listen to and stop listening to it. Once you identify it, then it will go away. If it tells you to do something that is not good, you know that it is not the voice. For example, if you have an addiction, and a voice tells you to feed the addiction, then it is not the right voice.

The one that comes with you, the one that is right beside you, is the one talking to you all the time. At first, it seems like it's far away. However, once you learn to listen to it, you will hear it more clearly and recognize it.

When I heard the voice, I knew it was there to help and guide me. Those were the words to follow. You have a deep trust and understanding because you know. If they came from that place, if you follow those words, you have nothing to worry about. Even if I am shipwrecked right in the middle of the ocean, and there's nothing around me, and that voice says, "Don't worry," but my logical mind asks, "how can I not worry?" Because I was at that place, and I know that voice, I would breathe with balance, float with balance, and be aware with balance. Therefore, when that big stick or ocean debris passes me, I will see it, get on it, and then I will rest until the time comes for me to be rescued. That is how powerful this is.

So how do you know the difference between that voice and your own voice?

Because I heard it. How do you hear it? You just have to open yourself up to hear it. Then you know when it is trying to communicate with you. When you're clear that what you heard on the inside you experienced on the outside, you learn to trust. And then once you trust, you maintain faith, humility, and patience because you know that, from that day forward. You now have to continue a life that challenges your ego not to take on things independently.

However, you must first learn to listen to that voice.

3

Words Are Alive

Words vibrate. One word might make the sound duuunnnnnng; like hitting a bell. Another word might make the sound, dooonnnnng, while another word might make the sound, diiiinnnnnng. That is how words grow. However, if you have words (dung, dung, dung) that are the same, they are just going to stay the same. If there are different sounds, they bounce off each other and become different and grow. And they go in you and grow inside you.

Words stimulate your organs; they stimulate your colon, pancreas, stomach, heart, and other parts of your body from head to toe. You do not even have to read them out loud. All you need is to say them in your mind. When you say them in your mind, they vibrate. They not only have an outward vibration, but they also have an inward vibration.

Words have been changed from their original language. They have been taken and reconfigured, reconstructed, and made flat. Living words have dimensions to them 3-D, 5-D, and 7-D. The pyramid walls are important because they contain words in a language that travels faster and has a higher sequence of tones. Indigenous people can capture them just by looking at them because their minds can see and read them. You may not be able to say them because your tongue is not trained in that manner, but your mind can read them, and they talk to you. It is not external; it is internal.

When you put words together, like atoms, they bump into each other when you say them, outwardly or inwardly. When they bump into each other, based on the configuration of the shape, they vibrate and have a tone. Together they have a certain frequency that gives them life. That is why it is said that words are alive; they may be fixed on your paper, but they are alive. When they bump into each other, certain word connections, certain word sequences, give different sounds. The sequences create something different and they morph into something inside you. When this happens, your organs hear them because they translate them into their own language; everything has its own language.

If you were trying to be politically correct, for example, you might use words in which the intent is to program you to conform. Thus, the word forms may lack growth and power. It is called numbing them down. Therefore, all I will get out of this sequence is ummmm (a sound said with a lower and less powerful tone). But if I go to my native language, I will get Um, Um, Um (a sound said with a more powerful and rhythmic tone).

Words bring you into them, into their reality. When you have done the work and are open, you will be able to hear them, how they talk, and what they say. The problem is people can't hear what the words are really saying. That's why they say there is always a backstory to everything because, in many cases, they say something totally different from what you are hearing. They are saying something different. When you know that, you can hear that. When you know that you can smile in every situation, you will never be rattled because you can hear what the words are really saying.

There were moments when words needed to talk to you, to let you know when you were facing danger, and the right words to say in certain situations. Words from some of these experiences are still vibrating inside you, and they will remain with you and talk to you. It is what we call memory. We are constantly filming with our eyes and recording with our ears. These films and recordings make up our memory catalog. Words live there and are alive. They will come back up in certain sequences with other words and deliver a message based on your memory catalog.

The memory catalog may be stagnant, but the imagination is boundless. Good words with the power and strength of the imagination have a different vibration. Those who use the right words with the power of imagination can bring things into manifestation. Some call this magic.

Words are like a 3-D printer. What makes a 3-D printer so great is that the codes it is coded with bounce together, develop a sequence of vibrations, and make a form. It is the same thing with words and the imagination; they can bring things into manifestation; they can bring things into form.

Messages to the True Descendants

Words talk to you internally; they speak to you. They stimulate parts of your mind, body, and being. They stimulate you deep down in your soul; a soul that has traveled from the beginning of time, where source lies and is alive.

Words have the power to unlock the source of all sources that lives inside of you.

4

The Moment

Some of us have had experiences that have become locked into our memory, causing us to be stuck in the past. Because we are stuck in the past, we are blocked, and this makes it difficult to live in the moment. When you are stuck in the past, you miss whatever you're supposed to gain at that moment. You miss the opportunity of what that moment has to offer.

For example, you might meet a good person. But because you're stuck on past bad memories, you are blocked from seeing the person for who he or she is. Because your memories are based on negative experiences you have had, you think this person will treat you the way the person in your past relationship did, and you miss the opportunity.

So the question is, "How do you want to live your life? Do you want to live in the moment to get what you need from the experience of that moment?" The moment is fresh and new. That means that what you get from source is fresh and new. You haven't experienced what source has for you yet. It is only in the moment that you will experience what is for you at that moment, and what you need for the future.

While you do not want to live in the past, it is important to know the past. If you do not know the past, you cannot see the future and will have difficulty living in the moment. When you know the past, you can see the future, and this helps you live in the moment. It is important to know the past to live in the moment and evolve into whoever you are to become in the future.

When you live in the moment, you will truly see yourself and who you can become.

5

Bending Space and Time

I wanted to get to a certain destination, but I had two roads I could take to get there at a particular time. I could take the left road and left turn or take the right road and turn right.

As I came around the corner towards my destination, I saw my son, who I was going to see, driving to the back of the building. As I got to the corner, the end of the building allowed me to see that he was driving away. The front of the building looked like nobody was there; as if it was closed. However, he was there and was driving to the back of the building.

If I had taken the left turn, I would have gotten there three minutes later and would have never seen him drive away. I would not have known that he was there and kept going and missed him. If I had taken the left turn, I would have only seen the front of the building and kept going. But the way I came in, I saw him, and we pulled right beside each other.

As soon as I pulled up, he said, "Wow, pops, your timing is impeccable." I said, "Yeah, man. I chose the right road. You see, if I had taken a left, I would have missed you. The right, I got you." I took the right turn, and I got exactly where I needed to be in the exact space and time.

I can look through curves and see things that most people cannot see. What I am seeing are curvatures of time, bending space. For example, when we were in Rome, I saw a light beam coming up through the ground in front of the obelisk at St. Peter's Basilica in Vatican City. I pointed it out, but you (speaking to the writer), could not see it. I took out my cell phone and took a picture and captured it. Then you were able to see it. Time was bending space that brought about a curvature that showed a light allowing us to see the power of the obelisk. It opened a space in time just for us to see it.

It is the same thing with your life. When you are born, the universe opens space and time for you to create. Your life is your God-given space and time to create. Bending is using your God-given birthrights of space and time to create what you want to get out of it; the life you choose. What do you create? You create your own world; you create how you want your world to look.

There are certain times that you are supposed to do things that the universe opens a space in time for you. If you are really in tune and focused when trying to get a job done, you will be given a curvature of space and time. Then you can create what you want to create or build whatever you want to build. Whether you are trying to build upon your character, your participation with others, or whatever it is, you are given space and time to do so, and it works like magic.

When the curvature of space and time opens, you will miss it if you don't catch it, and you will miss the opportunity. That's why it is said that timing is everything. If you don't catch the opportunity at the right time, you will miss it.

We all can bend space and time, but we allow things to interfere. We may have a moment of doubt, discouragement, weakness, or a sidebar conversation with someone and think it is better than our own. It slows you down and throws you off track.

Do not allow things to interfere and miss the opportunity of space and time to do what you want to do and create what you want to create.

Use your God-given space and time to get out of this life what you want to get out of it. Use your space and time to create your own world and the kind of world you want to live in.

6

Defying Gravity

In a movie that I watched, one of the characters said, "My takeaway is this, you defy gravity because gravity is not pulling you down. But gravity is supposed to pull you down. So how are you doing that?" The other character responded, "If you are true to your heart, and you are clear in your understanding, and you accept the reality that gravity is a force in and of itself, it will assist you. If you accept that balance is a force in and of itself, it will assist you. Then you will defy the odds of gravity pulling you down because they will assist you and help you go up; they will help you rise."

That was profound because all the character knew was the Western understanding of gravity. The only thing he knew is that gravity pulls you down. He responded, "Well, that's true. I'm not going to jump off a building. But I will do things within my ability and ask for the assistance of gravity, and I will ask for the assistance of balance to help me do things."

It was ironic to hear that in the movie because it was the same philosophy I had just given my grandson. Before seeing the movie, I saw him when I brought some heavy items to his house. I told my grandson, you are fifteen. Now you must learn and understand how to work with the forces, which means nothing is too heavy.

If you understand that gravity and balance are intelligent forces, and you are true to that, you can ask for their assistance. Then gravity and balance in your mind will offset what is heavy so that it won't be heavy anymore. If you are true to your heart and true in your truths, the elements; air, earth, water, and fire, will assist you on your journey and in everything you do. The forces of nature will work with you. But you must be true to yourself and true to the reality of that. The assistance only comes exactly as you ask for it. It only comes to those who are clear about the existence of the many independent, intelligent forces that are around us but are invisible to the eye.

If you have that understanding and deep belief, dive deep into that philosophy at a young age, and let it grow on you until you become mature, you will have that relationship and that reality. It will work like magic because that's how magic works. If you embrace that truth down to the core of your being, then there is nothing out there that can convince you otherwise that this is not real.

Michael Jordan received his gift from the god of gravity. The god of gravity wanted to show us that man can defy gravity. The god of gravity recognized Michael Jordan because he sat still long enough to listen, believed with all his heart, and practiced. Because he listened, believed, and practiced, the god of gravity granted him his request. That is why he was able to stay in the air longer than any man we know of other than a spaceman. He proved it by staying in the air longer than any other basketball player known to man, thus far.

If I had known about the elements and how this thing works at a younger age, I cannot imagine where I would be today. I could not imagine that I had that kind of power as a human being walking this earth; that I have the alliance and the technology to talk to the elements to help me in my journey. This knowledge has been known throughout the world. A few use it to their advantage, but many of us do not know this. We do not know how the elements can assist you and the truth of how they operate on the planet.

Ancient people knew because they were in touch with nature. And some people know today, but because of where we live, we are out of touch with nature, and therefore do not focus on it.

In America, we learn what we are taught in the education system. Imagine if you grew up in societies that teach these things from an early age. We are so far removed from the reality of how nature works. Many do not grasp it until a certain stage in life after they slow down. Then there is not enough life left in the body to learn these things to the depth you could if you started earlier.

However, you can defy that too if you catch it soon enough and eat all the right foods. You need to manage what you eat and avoid putting artificial foods in your body. Eat the things of the planet because you become what you eat. If you eat the elements, you will become them because they are inside you. What is outside is inside. If you eat what you are made of, it will be your reality, and you will hear it when it speaks to you because you are made of it.

You are nurturing what you are already made of. If you are eating foods that are not naturally what you are made of it will affect you in different ways, which we are seeing play out in how people think that seem way out of touch with reality.

You are building upon your foundation. If you are building a foundation with wood or brick and mortar, that will stand strong. But if you are laying a foundation full of things that dissolve or crumble, you will eventually crumble.

We all can defy gravity. We all have the ability to work with the elements and forces of nature. And we are all born with gifts. The level to which we can bring these gifts into manifestation is a function of our willingness to listen, remain steadfast in our practice, and believe with all our hearts.

Do this, and the gods will recognize you and grant you their gifts.

7

Crushed by a Rock

A person may be in pain, and they forget about it. Then someone might ask, "How are you doing?" They remind you that you are supposed to be in pain. Then the person says, "Oh, yeah, I remember." Then they feel the pain.

People remind you of how you are supposed to be. And then you remember. You say, "Oh, yeah, I forgot," while you are in the middle of lifting a heavy rock. Someone reminds you that the rock is heavy and breaks you out of your trance, and then the rock becomes heavy. They throw you off because they broke your trance. Then you get crushed by the rock because you allowed yourself to be absorbed into someone else's reality. You allowed someone else's reality to come in the middle of yours.

They say you cannot climb the Rock of Gibraltar. But you can. If you stay in trance, you can subdue it, and some men have. You may be an athlete and are doing a triathlon, where you have to run, cycle and swim ten miles. You are swimming, and suddenly someone starts talking to you, and you lose your trance.

I know that because I used to cycle. When you are doing 100-mile, 150-mile cycles, you go into a trance. That is when your third eye kicks in because it has the vision of the future. You are racing towards the future. However, once you get knocked off your vision of the future, you can only see where you are now. Therefore, if you are in the middle of swimming and have five more miles to go, it is hard to get back into the third eye vision of the future because you're so tired. You could see the future because that is where you were headed. But if you get knocked off that, if you lose the heat of the moment, you will not make it because you lost focus.

Everybody has their reality. The problem is that we can no longer hear it because there is so much noise in the world. We get drawn into all the noise. We cannot maintain our equilibrium because we are always getting drawn into someone else's reality.

If you stay in your own reality; if you stay focused and stay on track, you won't get crushed by the rock.

8

Once You Know Then You Know

We see, hear, and experience everything. But because some of it is so profound, it is scary. It is so unlike what you have been taught in your educational system. However, you will assess and attach something you learned in the educational system or your memory to take away from what you know you experienced.

For example, you know that big old giant with the deep, scary voice that spoke to you in a language you never heard before, is there. But you do not know how to handle it. If you hold on to what you experienced, if you hold on to what you know you saw, felt, heard; if you do that, it is too difficult. And you cannot live life like that. Because once you know, then you know, and you are on the alert for it for the rest of your life. And who wants to be on alert?

In some of the stories, like in the story of Moses, for example, some went beyond the gate and saw things that we have never seen before. Some forces ensured that those generations who knew what they experienced, all the elders who had the true stories; perished. So, the generations down just heard the elders' stories; folklore, but they did not truly understand what they experienced. Now it is called allegory, but some of the experiences are real.

It is both. One side is stories that are designed to teach moral lessons and facilitate our journey into the self. There is, however, the other side that has to do with all the things going on outside of the self. Some say that the stories are made up—that they are mythological, but some are true. It is both. Those who say that the stories are myths do not take into consideration, that which is passed down from mouth to ear that only a few are privy to know.

Some people think that everything they read in religious books is based on true experiences. They do not know that some are not. Some are merely messages; secret codes. It gets back to the law of polarity. With the law of polarity, the pendulum goes both ways. It swings to the right, and it swings to the left. It is like the North Pole and the South Pole. They are the poles of polarity. In the middle is the core, the balance.

To get to the truth, you have to understand both sides. You have the truth, and you have the allegory. It is your job to find the middle place, not to get so stuck that you become blind. You must always be open. If you are stuck to the right of the truth or the left of allegory, you will miss something. If you stay in the middle, you can discern what is truth and what is an allegory because it's all about learning to be a better person. It's about having a better understanding and being prepared for moments that you will face in your life journey.

Everything is about evolution. It's about continuously growing and not becoming stuck. If you stay true to the spirit, you will continue to grow, see, have experiences, and even create and develop things that you never thought possible. If you know that the spirit exists, you know that you have assistants who can help get you what you need, if you can get beyond self, that blocks you.

9

What Dreams Are

I had a dream that I was in the presence of other people living with them and was involved in their lives completely. They saw and accepted me with no separation. In my memory, before I went to bed, I was the image of myself. The only thing I know is that this is me, in a dream that I do not belong in because I am not in a relationship with any of the characters in my dream. Because I do not belong there, it caused a separation in my mind.

But then, as I was in this dream, engaging with these people in personal conversations, with acceptance, and everything else, I was walking with them and passed a mirror. I looked in the mirror, and the image that I saw in the mirror was not the image of me. Only in my mind was it me. I was not the image I saw in the mirror. I said, "Oh, that's why they accept me. It's not me!" At that moment, I realized I was in someone else's body. I was visiting in the spiritual form as another presence. I took over that body, and I was experiencing his experiences through my conscious thoughts in the dream state. But it was not me. I was just having these experiences in someone else's body.

The image in the mirror was not me, but I was participating in this life. That is why the characters were so real. You could not have thought of these experiences before going to bed. They are fresh new experiences because you are experiencing them in another body you entered into while in the dream state. Then you come back to your body, and that life continues. You just took over someone else's body.

You went out in the world, entered another body, looked through their eyes, experienced their life, and then you came back to bed. Their default mechanism then went back into full play, and they continued to go on with life as usual. Because I had an experience that I know was real, and I did not know anything about what the character was going through before going to bed, I must have been in someone else's life. I did not know that until I looked in the mirror and said, "This is not me!"

We are out of touch with our dreams because we only view them through the person we were before going to bed; our body, mind, looks, and attributes. But in some cases, it is not you who is in the dream. You took over someone else's body. Those in the dream are interacting with and talking to that person, not you. I now understand that.

When you go to bed, a part of you goes through dark space and travels to different places in the universe. When you are in a dream with a big old monster chasing you, he is not chasing you. You just happened to visit another creature that happens to be food or prey for that creature that is chasing you. If you pass a mirror, you will see that you look like an old ugly beast. You are in its body. You have to jump off when you get to the edge because this creature has to jump off the edge to save himself from the monster. You then come back to your body. You thought it was you the creature was chasing; it was not. You were just in another body going through what the creature had to experience in its lifetime.

Messages to the True Descendants

When you go to different places in the universe, it is not you who goes there, it is a part of you that enters into another form and endures and sees the experiences that person, creature, or whatever it is, is going through, and you think that it is who you are in your conscious mind. But it isn't. And then you leave it and come back to your body.

It is confusing because the only thing you know about what happened to you is in your physical body that knows that you do not belong there. This is what causes the disconnect. This is why we do not accept or receive these experiences or forget about them because they are not true to us. It is not you in the physical form. It is just a part of you experiencing another creature that lives in the universes we participate in.

I only found out because I encountered a mirror that was not supposed to be there, and I looked at it, and I saw it. They screwed up. There are supposed to be no mirrors when we have these experiences.

Why are we having these experiences?

The part of you that leaves when you are sleeping is trying to communicate with you. It has an antenna or a connector. When it's out in the dream world having these experiences, it is also downloading data into your conscious so that you can see what's in your future.

If you don't listen to what it has been trying to tell you, then maybe you'll see what it shows you. And then when you wake up, you come back and say, "What was that about?" "Oh, I've been here before, or I've seen this before." It is trying to communicate something to you. If it cannot communicate with you or if you will not listen, then it will go out into the night, the dream world, and try to show you.

They download the information into your brain, and then what?

So that when you wake up, you'll see what spirit is trying to tell you. There are two means of communication. One is inside of you talking, from your subconscious to your conscious. And when that doesn't work, it has to use your superconscious to go out and show you what it is trying to tell you or what your future looks like. A part of you leaves in the night and shows you what the spirit is trying to tell you. You wake up, and say, "I had this dream about this or that."

But most of us don't understand what our dreams are trying to tell us.

After you read this, you will begin to be more conscious; you will pay closer attention to your dreams. You ask, "How can I pay attention to something that I cannot connect to my reality?" But now that you are aware that your dreams are a reality, you'll begin to listen, learn more, do better, and have a better understanding. Your dreams will then become clearer as time goes on. When the information is stored in your memory, you will have an important pile and a junk pile.

When you are aware of this reality, you'll begin to go to bed with something intentional on your mind. Then your spirit will show you where it is or what it is. It will tell you whether you need to move toward or away from it, whether you need to accept something or leave it alone. When you get better at this, you will go straight to the important pile, and you will remember that and be better at deciphering what it is trying to show you.

But first, you must know that dreams are a part of reality. They are a part of you, your life, and your future.

10

Genie Out of the Bottle

When you are conceived, your genes are imprinted with your genius (creative power, ability, and gifts), and you are given an assistant, popularly known as a genie, to accompany you on earth. Its role is to help bring your genius into manifestation and carry out your purpose.

Your genie is under the command of your voice that is connected to source. However, because many of us lose our voice, we lose the power to command our genie, and it thinks it can get away with things and goes rogue. That's what is meant by letting the genie out of the bottle. The bottle is you, and your genie is the presence that helps bring your genius to manifestation.

Messages to the True Descendants

A genie that is no longer under the command of the voice can go rogue and wreak havoc on the world. It can even go rogue in the night when you are asleep. Then it says, "Oh, I have to go back home," and jumps back in you. When you're sleeping, when you are dormant, it is wreaking havoc all over the universe.

When your genie goes rogue, it stays out there until you recognize that you can no longer hear your voice. Once you hear your voice again, you can use it to bring your genie back under your control. Because we're so caught up in the machine culture, we don't know that our voice is being blocked by voices from external sources. You don't know that your genie is out, that it's out doing its thing. It is what you call doing your thing.

That is why the parent tells the child to come in at dusk when the streetlights come on. They want to know that their child is home and safe so that they will have control of them. They want to make sure the genie inside their child doesn't go rogue and bring their child down roads that can harm him. It is a subconscious understanding. When your genie is out in the night, it roams the streets, looking for opportunity. When it sees an opportunity, it tells the child, "I want you to see if you can break into that store and get those clothes out of there" or "break into that house." The child does it and has that experience. From that day forward, the child has bad ideas about breaking into houses, businesses, cars, etc. That experience stimulates a whole strain of wrong ideas and leads to other misdeeds.

If the child had gone into the house at dusk, he would have never gotten the rush, feeling, and vibration of the genie who got satisfied by going rogue. Once you get that feeling, once you get a taste of that, your ego takes over and makes you want to keep doing whatever it is.

What you get in the moment of that experience is the feeling and the power of the endorphins and the adrenalin that rushes through your body. It's a natural high. You want that feeling over and over again. It was stimulated by the feeling that the genie got when it did that. And you don't know that it wasn't even you.

Those who know that it wasn't them, go home and say, "Oh, I'll never do that again because that wasn't me." But no parent wants to take that risk. That's why they say, "I want you in this house before the streetlights come on. When it's dusk, I want you in this house." Because a genie in the night with no restrictions can go rogue, and the child becomes prey to bad ideas, bad influences, and bad situations, all of which lead to a bad return. The child's genius is exploited by human and spirit predators, who roam the streets at night and influence the child because they want to use his genius to their benefit.

Are there some good genies? Can you let the good genie out of the bottle?

The positive-minded person may let the genie out the bottle intentionally to seek out the answers he's looking for. You tell the genie exactly what you want, and it goes out and grants you your wish. So you let the genie out of the bottle. This is what happens when there is a positive integration between your voice and your genie. Many miss out on their dreams, gifts, and purpose because they are not listening to their voice that has the oversight and power of God Almighty.

Messages have been coming down to tell us what's going on since we were children, about containing your genie. Cartoons and movies have been telling us that when a genie goes rogue, he becomes a bad person in the world. They say you get three wishes, and the genie will grant them for you. They say three because they try to keep you contained and under control. Because if you knew you had unlimited wishes, then you would know your power. However, it can be dangerous if you use these powers in ways that people are using them today—for selfishness, greed, ego, etc. So they try to limit them to keep you contained. But the power of your genie is unlimited.

What your genius can manifest is unlimited. It depends on the stage of your life journey and how much time you have left before you will have a clear understanding of this. Once you learn about this, they know that there is only so much time left for you to wreak havoc. Eventually, your life will end, your body will return to the earth, and your spirit will be recycled.

So basically, physical death is a way to stop anyone from having too much power for too long?

Messages to the True Descendants

Yes, that stops you. You go back. Either you get it right, and they let you live in the spirit world and assist with the creation and development of humanity, or you come back and start all over again. You reset.

Because people have so much power, it prevents them from keeping it going too long. Their descendants may keep it going. But they have to get that one out. There is always the possibility that their descendants might not continue the bad they are bringing.

Yes. They have to get that one out. When you get to a place where even the generational line gets out of control, then that generational line is eventually extinguished. You are no more, and you get recycled, and you'll be waiting for another opportunity to start a whole new line.

11

It is in the Numbers

You have to be good on your axis. Your life has to add up to certain numbers to be on your axis.

—Are you doing the right thing?
—Is your word your bond?

If your answers to these questions are affirmative, your numbers are going to be good. For example, if your word is good 98 percent of the time, those are good numbers. You are going to get 100 percent from the universe because it knows you are a good person. If it is right for humanity—good on the human level, it means you will be solid on your axis because your axis is online, and you can balance out what is not so good.

Messages to the True Descendants

If you only do 30 percent of what you say, your numbers will be off, and your axis will be off. When something bad comes your way, it will hit you because you are off your axis.

—Words equal numbers

—Emotions equal numbers

—Attitude equals numbers

—Thoughts equals numbers

—Actions equals numbers

What makes life hard for many people is that they are inconsistent. Averages are the key. If your numbers are off by ten years, you must have ten years of doing good to make up for it. No matter where you are, you can start at any point. It is never too late. If the numbers are right, your axis will be right, and you can repel any bad that comes your way.

Your axis will be just that powerful. You will be powerful enough to pick up your sister or brother and carry them on your back. You will be able to do just that.

If you want to be in a relationship with someone, questions you should ask going in are:

—Who are you?

—How good is your word?

—What are your intentions?

—How well do you treat your family?

—How well do you comply with society's rules?

We think lust is love. That is what society tells us. It makes us think lust is love. Lust can help love grow, but it is not the rudiment of love. If you understand love, you will know that it encompasses all these things.

If the person you are trying to attract has numbers like yours, you will subliminally see each other. You will see them in your auras. If your numbers are not good, you are not going to be good, and your relationship will not be good.

If your numbers are good, the universe will do the rest.

12

We Are in the Dark

We are in the dark. You think that you are burying your secrets in the dark, but you are not. You are only handing them to us because that is where we are.

It is written that in the beginning, I created the world from the dark. So where do you think I am? I came from the dark to the light. From the dark, I created everything that is. From the dark, I delivered a soul to live in harmony.

From the dark we became.
In the dark is where we are.

There are no secrets. We know everything that you do.

The vibrations of negative thoughts and words stimulate forces in other realms in space and time. These forces come into the world through souls; they travel through souls. They come in through your thoughts and words of affliction. When they come in, you are no longer capable of controlling your actions. Because your eyes are open, you think that it is you, but it is not. You are in a trance. Then after you have done something you should not have done, you don't know what came over you; you are remorseful and have to apologize.

Using drugs (including alcohol) makes you vulnerable to forces in other realms in space and time. They put you in a trance, a dormant state so that a traveler can take over. Depending on the drug, they have different effects on different people. In some people, they bring insight and wisdom; they are the special ones. For others, they bring chaos. That is why permitting the widespread use of drugs is dangerous.

In the past, only the spiritual divine man had access to them. Only shamans, priests, diviners, etc., had access to mind-altering drugs. They had to prove they were worthy. They had to go through years of training, and show that they were of good moral character, had good intentions, and were going to use them for good. They also had to show that they could handle them before they were given access to them. They would use them to travel to other dimensions and bring back information needed for the people.

But now, everybody has access to drugs and alcohol, and things are out of control because nobody knows what is happening to them. This is because their eyes are open. As long as their eyes are open, they think they are conscious.

Past experiences may flare up when you are angry or in certain situations, and you have negative thoughts. When this happens, a traveler can take over, and you do something that you should not do. It is internal afflictions that may stimulate a different character one takes into the night. A person may be sitting home, and suddenly, something happens. Now he is in the streets trying to rob and kill somebody. Then he goes to bed and wakes up and says, "Oh, my God, I did that?" Now the world is looking for him.

We have the power to unlock the doors that allow other forces to help you. And these forces have the key to unlock certain mechanisms that are a part of your make-up. When we are needed, you can call upon us, and we will help you. But you must know that we are here.

For some forces that work through the human body, if they realize you see them, they will leave. The problem is when you see a crazy man, you won't look him in the eyes, you run. However, if you look him in his eyes, he will look at you and say, "Oh, man. I didn't mean it; man, you know..." He will talk out of his head for a minute and go on about his way. Some people can see those with bad intentions in the eyes of people. When you see them, they flee because they do not want to be seen.

Whenever someone is in jeopardy, we have the power to call on forces based on the source of the problem. We call on the hierarchy. Some of these forces rule the elements; earth, air, water, and fire. They can use the elements to help you.

You must know that we are here. And we are in a space that you cannot see. Everybody must have this understanding and be aware of that. If you are aware of this, you will be cautious of the things you do. Nothing can creep up on you and make you do something you should not do. When you are aware that we see everything you do, you will make sure that what you do is good because there is a price to pay. You must be aware that all the things you put out in the world will be in there with you, and we are watching you.

We will always be in the dark. You cannot see us because we occupy a space that you cannot see. You cannot see us because your eyes are not designed to see in the dark. Because you cannot see us, you will never be as powerful as we are. We are always faster, stronger, and smarter than you.

We see you, but you cannot see us.

13

The Curve

The ego is powered by the unlimited source of the will. It can help you navigate and get through conflicts, confusion, and difficulties you encounter. It tells you, "I can." It says, "Don't worry, we can do this." It says, "We can get through this, overcome that, create this or become that." But there is a flip side to the ego.

The other side is when it has convinced the "I can," that is driven by selfishness, greed, lust, deception, etc., secrets that people think nobody knows because they are smiling. But all along, they have something different in mind. They think that you can't see them, and a lot of people do not because the ego is smart. Some are sharp based on their practice.

However, some people do see them. When you see them, you can attempt to help them. All you have to do is look them in their eyes. When they know you know what is driving them, they will try to control it as long as possible; sometimes it's five minutes, 15 minutes, an hour; sometimes it's five days, a week, or even a year. Those who are sincere will change their ways. But those who are not, whatever is driving their ego will come back out.

Egotistical people think they are in control. However, they are never in control because there is always a curve. They don't know where the curve is or when it's coming, but it's coming. Because they are moving too fast, when they hit the curve, they are going to get wiped out.

It's not a matter of whether there is a curve, it's a matter of where it is and when it is coming. The curve is inevitable.

There is going to be a day of reckoning. There is going to be a day when you will face that curve. You need to change your ways before that day comes. You want to change your ways before you come to that curve because hitting it has two potential outcomes. It can just kick your butt so bad that you suffer from having to live with one foot, one arm, or one eye, causing you to live the rest of your life in misery. All you will say from that day forward is, "I should not have done that." The other outcome is, it wipes you out completely and you come face-to-face with the doorway, and then you're not allowed in and have come back and do it all over again.

The only ones that go around the curve are those who hear the words that come down in flashes of seconds the moment you face it. You come to the curve, catch the words, and listen at that time because it takes that to wake you up.

Those who listen and change before that; those who slow down enough to see the curve coming can prevent hitting it. They will go around the curve and get through it. They start stacking the numbers so they can say, "I am worthy and protected. I'm covered and I can get through this. My generational line will continue to be a recipient of my change."

Everyone is going to face a curve. Will you hit it and have to deal with thirty years of misery? Will you hit it and that means your time on the planet is over?

Messages to the True Descendants

The question is not whether you will come to a curve, it's a question of when you do, will you be able to glide around it gracefully.

14

The Crappy Ones

Some of the spirits are crappy. They are nasty, ugly, stinky, and try to stick on you because they don't want to go. You can see them sometimes when you see people doing crappy things. What they are thinking are not even their thoughts. The thoughts come in through the hollow space of the crappy ones. You can see the residue of the crap some people create that has evolved from comingling with the energy of others. The crappy ones just wreak havoc. That's all they do. All they do is cause chaos.

What do they get out of that?

Joy? They love it. That's their joy.

So, where do they come from?

Different corners, different regions of time and space.

People will ask the question that if God created everything, did God create the crappy ones?

There are different sectors. The universe is vast. It is so vast that you can't imagine how vast it is. We must accept the reality that our minds can go but so far. Its vastness goes beyond what our minds can understand. It is vast, and there is more than one. This is our region. And in our region, we got the baddest of the baddest of all of them. They are on record of being the baddest of the baddest.

When you say we have the baddest, are you saying they deal with the crappy ones?

It is raising your vibration that gets rid of the crappy ones. You have an external source, and you have an internal source. The internal source that every man has as a true descendant will feel the vibration of the power when they read these words. After reading these words, they will begin to grow inside of you. It's like going to the cabinet and getting some cough medicine and taking a spoonful to get rid of your sickness. That's what happens in this case. The vibration of these words will stimulate the cleansing process that will cleanse the crap from you. So, the big boys don't need to deal with this. The big boys don't need to deal with stuff on this level; it's petty.

Are you saying that when someone does something crappy, there are beings to help get rid of the crap?

They are there to make sure the crap doesn't cause too much harm or wreak so much havoc, that it makes this thing go off-kilter. Some things occur to challenge man. That's how man evolves. That's how he overcomes things. However, they have to make sure that it doesn't get too far over the edge. So when things happen, there's a call to order to those protected and sanctioned by higher powers. They have to stand in for you in front of them. Because that's how bad they are, they are chosen for that purpose.

So you are saying those are the ones that make sure things don't get out of control?

Yes, they are chosen for that purpose. They are sanctioned by higher powers. When they bless you, you get all the blessings from all the powers and elements along the way. All the elements will give you grace and mercy. When you know this, you will know how to call on him (your internal source), who is the link to them (your external sources).

Who is him?

The one who comes with you. It is the voice inside of you that everybody knows is there but does not know is there. Because we do not know in our conscious mind that it is there, we do not listen to it. Therefore, we do not know its power. If you listen and let it guide you, you will know its power. Once you know its power, you can rid yourself of the crappy stuff, and you won't abuse it.

That's the key. How to get you to know and embrace your power and not abuse it. When you know that, that's it.

16

Sitting in the Bathroom

People make bad decisions in a moment and get stuck in that moment. They do not want to wait for a long time to get out of it. However, they better get used to where they are because they are not going anywhere and may be there for a very long time. It can take thousands of years because, in that place, time stands still.

I found this out because I was in a place, and a presence was there. A group of souls was passing through, and I asked, "Well, how long have I been here? How long have I been asleep, an hour, two hours, two days?" And it said, "No. Dude, you have been asleep for ten years. You have been here for ten years." I thought I was only in there for a short time, but ten years had passed.

While attempting to keep me cool, the presence gingerly explained to me what I had to wait for. Then it left, and it left me sitting in that bathroom. It left me sitting there, and I recognized that I would be there for a long time. At that moment, I realized I was dead. I did not know I was dead before then. When I woke up from my sleep, I looked out the window and walked into the bathroom to make sure I did not die in my sleep.

That is how I caught that message so clearly. If you cannot get through the gate, you will be stuck in places like that for a long time.

To get through the door, you must pay attention to your numbers. You must make sure your numbers are right. For example, if you have 40 years of negative numbers, you will need 40 years to bring them back to zero. If you need to get on a fast track, you must double the numbers to make it 20 years or triple the numbers to make it ten years. You will need to increase your numbers to make sure you can get through the gate.

If those numbers do not add up, you are not going to get through, and you will be stuck in that bathroom, that pit, or that burning car. You will think that you have gotten out of that body, but that body will be sitting with you because you did something 40 years ago. You will be stuck in the presence of that nasty body that you mutilated before you went down. You will be sitting with it for a long time. You thought you got away with the wrong things you did, but you are not getting away with anything. If the numbers do not add up, you may be with whatever it is for what seems like eternity. You must increase your numbers.

You are racing against time, and the clock is ticking.

15

You Are Not Going to Heaven

For six days a week, you are selfish, greedy, dishonorable, disrespectful, judgmental, lustful, deceitful, foul-mouthed, engage in gossip, and worship false gods (social media and other things of the machine culture). You treat your children badly and won't accept them and help them navigate through issues created by you. You kill your brother and you run and hide. And you think we don't see you. Then on the seventh day, you go to church and pray. And you think you are going to heaven.

If you don't get it right here, you will not have the opportunity to get it right there. We do not have time to see when you get to heaven whether you are going to do right. So don't think you're going to heaven because you apologize the day that you are dying. You are not going to heaven. If you don't live it on earth, we are not taking a chance on you in heaven. There is no forgiveness if you don't prove who you are while you are here.

This is where the confusion is and why people live carelessly up until the day they're on their deathbed. Then they say, "Oh, I apologize. Please forgive me. I accept Jesus Christ as my Lord and Holy Savior." Sorry, it's too late. We don't have time for that now because you're lying now, and you'll be lying when you get there. We are not taking that chance. There is no schooling there. You either are or you aren't. If you are, you will be allowed in. If you aren't, you will not get in.

You are not going to heaven, because you're just fake and you're false and you think we don't see you. You think we don't know. But we do. That's the deal.

17

My Boys

I see and hear everything that goes on. And I got my boys with me. My boys are rough and tough, and they are mean. They will cuss, they hit you, and they will kick you. My boys will jam you; they will mess you up. They will make you get the point because we are not playing.

My boys are serious. And I am sending them; I am sending my boys out now. That is what is happening. They are being unleashed to clean up the mess that you are making.

>My boys are in the ocean that can bring
>>down the mightiest of the mighty.
>My boys are in the rain that pours
>>unceasingly.
>My boys are in the thunder and lightning
>>that bang and crack the earth.

Messages to the True Descendants

My boys are in the fire that burns
    mercilessly.
My boys are in the rivers that can rise
    higher and run faster than
    anything you can create.
My boys are in the earth that shakes up
    things unrelentingly.
My boys are in the winds that form
    tornadoes and hurricanes that rip
    through cities and towns,
    uncompromisingly.

That's who I'm talking about. Those are my boys, and they are watching you.

And I am not talking about the boys in the hood. I am not talking about the boy with a 22-caliber gun running from the cops.

18

The Fourth Grade

Some people have not passed the fourth grade, but they want to keep company with those with a PhD, a doctorate in terms of how they think, act and behave and the contributions they are making to the world. Why would anyone with a doctorate want to be in the company of those who haven't passed the fourth grade? Those who cannot pass the fourth grade need to keep company with those who cannot pass the fourth grade.

The fourth grade here is the fourth dimension there. There are many people in the fourth dimension, and they are going to stay there. To get to the heavenly realms, you must get there while you are here. You must prove that you can do it here, then take it there. You will not be allowed to occupy a space with those who worked hard to go to the heavenly realms.

All of life has a filtering process. To get pure water, there is a filter that filters out all the debris. All the bad junk sits in the filter while the purified water passes through. It is the same with the heavenly realms. When you ascend upwards, there's a filter, and you will pass through that filter. That's what the fourth dimension is. It is a filter. It filters out the bad so that the pure can pass through.

If you have a lot of junk with you, you will not get through the filter because it is designed to stop you. If you cannot pass from the fourth grade here, you will not get past the fourth dimension there. Those without junk will flow on through. Those with junk will get stuck, and there's nothing they can do about it. No matter what you think, you are not getting through that filter. And you will be stuck in that filter because of the things you did while you were here.

If you think, act, and behave in ways that are not beyond the fourth grade, the question you must ask yourself is, why would anyone want to spend eternity with someone who couldn't pass the fourth grade? Why would they want to live an eternity of bliss, beauty, wonder, and awe with the freedom to roam the universe in peace with someone who doesn't have that privilege? They will be living the heavenly life while you will not be able to do so.

No one would be put in that position because they know that when you can't get what you want; when you can't have your way, you will try to wreak havoc there, and there is no havoc there.

The filtering process is pure, and it is precise.

21

The Report Card

As humans, we all come from pure source; God. We journey to earth to have an experience with the aim of returning to God. What we do while we are here determines where we return to and whether we come back here or not.

When you come back to repeat the journey, it depends on what realm you come back from. It is a selection process. Some come back because they still have lessons to learn to continue their evolvement back to source. Their situation or circumstances in this life has to do with how they lived and what they did in previous lifetimes.

When you come from certain realms, it means you have proven your goodness. Those who have done the most wonderful things are granted the gift of having the choice of coming back and having the human experience. However, once you are back here, you have to repel all the lust and the beauty of being involved in human flesh; that pulls you in and makes you make bad decisions.

It seems, if you get the opportunity to go to the heavenly realms, why would you want to come back here? Are you not taking a serious risk?

It is a beautiful thing because you're here to continue to create, produce, and procreate, to continue the growth and evolution of this planet, of this design.

So we come back here and risk screwing up?

We don't know that until we get here. That's the mystery. Before we get here, we're experiencing what it feels like to be in the bosom of God. We feel the wonders and the beauty and awe of being there in perfection.

I'm not clear. What are you saying?

I'll make it simple. When you want to hug someone, you don't know how beautiful it may feel until you hug them. If the energies integrate, the feeling, the level of weight, the level of height, all those things, you won't know how it feels until you hug them. Once you hug them, it feels good, and you don't want to leave.

It is the same thing with this human body on the planet that has a clock attached to it. You come down here and do your thing. And if you get it right and do what you're supposed to do, to help keep this thing going, you've done your part, your piece of this, what you are specialized to do. Everyone has a specialty, and there are many specialties.

So we are there. We come here. Some choose to come here because they want to help; others come back to get it right. But the goal is to get back there?

We come down here to do a job. When that body's time is up, when that clock is up, you have to go back. When you come here, you lose the memory of what it was like before you got here. You lose the memory of what you came here to do. That's where the voice comes in, it is there to guide you.

You're walking in the blind. The voice is guiding you into your awareness. And then when your awareness gets to that place, and you carry out your purpose, then when your body exterminates, you go back. However, if you don't listen to the voice that guides you because of the power of what we call the ego, it has its way and goes into overdrive and has the power to take over. Then that becomes the greater power.

The voice with you can command the elements here on the planet to help you deliver your purpose. The experience of the body has the vibration of godly presence that is so wonderful; we just don't want to leave it. We want to enjoy all the little things, the little nuances that come with the experience. And it delays you, screws you up, and takes you off track.

And then you start doing things that you shouldn't do.

Yes. Things that take you off track, off your course. You get stuck in something that you find so beautiful, so exhilarating, and you lose your way.

And then your clock runs out. Your time is up. Now you can't finish, you don't have time to get back on track.

It is why some people start to shut a lot of things down after a certain stage in life. You realize how far down some roads things can take you. That's why you're like, "No, no, no, no, I have to stop doing these things." That's why all religions teach you to detach from all the sensual things.

Right, you are supposed to do everything in moderation. But it depends on you and your purpose. So you can do some things in moderation; you just can't get stuck.

Those who want to have control stop doing things completely because they realize the roads they can take you down. You don't want to go down those roads because you know they're not good. That's the struggle. You try to balance, you try to do things in moderation, but that doesn't work. So some people go to the other extreme. You are so controlled that you are not living or experiencing all the beauty that this life has to offer.

The balance is off. So that's what it is about, getting that balance. It depends on your level of maturity and the level at which you understand reality. At the age of 20, it is hard. At age 30, it is hard. It may even be hard at 40 when you're peaking. That's when you understand what you have the power to do. And then you use it. Now the clock begins to go in the opposite direction.

So, what you did before the clock goes in the opposite direction will affect how you go through the rest of life. Did you use your life force in a balanced way, or did you burn it out?

The guarantee that's put in place is that you will only be able to enjoy this body for so long. Certain forces are going to make sure that happens.

You only have a certain amount of vitality; if you burn that vitality out early, you won't be here but so long. That is why people die early. You can burn it out in different ways. And it could be because you've got so involved in the lust of all the things that pull you; drugs, alcohol, sex, etc.

It could be too much education, a career, business, too much of anything that causes you stress.

Messages to the True Descendants

And now you get to a certain stage in the life cycle, and your time runs out because you burned out your life force prematurely.

That is the trick. Nobody knows when they are going to expire. So maybe you are supposed to burn out in education. Maybe you are supposed to burn out in drugs and alcohol; perhaps you're supposed to burn out. We don't know. It's all about the experience that brings the knowledge to understand that source is in everything. All of these things are something that must be known.

But we can control it. We can control how we use our life force and potentially our clock. I may experience using drugs, and now because I have had that experience, I can better help those suffering from addiction because I had the experience of it. However, once you use drugs, you're awakened to the downside of using drugs.

How would you know what to tell others to look out for? Unless you have that experience or see what it looks like and its results, you would not be able to tell them what to look out for and what to stay away from.

Messages to the True Descendants

I'm not saying you should not have the experience. People have experiences based on their purpose. What I am saying is that when you have an experience, it will tell you whether it is good or not. You have to listen to that voice that says this is not good. This is not working.

The voice says, "You've had enough." You got what it was supposed to deliver to you. You now know that experience, and you move on to the next. That class is over; you've graduated. But if you don't hear that and graduate, you'll get stuck, and your clock will be off. What you endured in the experience may not have been right, but it was right for the knowledge you gained.

I knew everything that I did that wasn't good for me because something told me that. Because of what it felt like. For example, when you use drugs or alcohol, there's a good side. You feel good, you're flying. But then there's the downside. When you come down, you feel bad. You lose time in the recovery period. At some point, you have to make a decision. Is the upside worth the downside? Is the high worth the low? The voice tells you it is not. But then you keep doing it anyway, you keep going down that road. Eventually, it is going to take you down and may eventually take you out. It's going to burn out your life force. So that's what I'm saying. Most of us know when we are doing something bad to our body because it will tell you, "That doesn't feel good." And you keep doing it and the voice nags you, "This isn't good. This isn't good." For some of us when this happens, whatever it is that we are doing, it's over.

Different things yield different results. If you look at where you are today, look at the gifts that you wished to receive but didn't get, or it is too late to get them; that's when you do your report card. Where you are and what your dream looks like, that's your report card. The only person that knows that is you. That's between you and the God Almighty.

That's another conversation.

No, it's the same conversation. It just tells you what was good and what wasn't. It equals the same thing.

If we look at our report card based on our dreams, some of us thought we were doing good, but we didn't get all the things we dreamed of. Things did not pan out the way we wanted them to. We got some things but didn't get them all. That is different from drinking, drugging, and eating foods that you know are poisonous to your body. And then you turn 50; now you're having a stroke because you continued to do things that were bad for your body. That is different than if you did things that were not good for society. It is a different report card.

It is a matter of what the report card is reporting. For example, in school, you get a grade in different subjects; math, science, English, social studies, etc. Then you get an average grade, and that is your final grade. It is the same for the report card for life.

Your report card for life tells you where you are in terms of your moral character and judgment, what good you are bringing to the world, and how you are using your God-given birthrights; the body you have been given, and the time and space you have been granted to create and carry out your purpose. When you have a report card that you check every so often, it helps determine where you are in your numbers and your grade. The problem is many people don't do the report card until it is too late. Then they don't have enough time to make up for it; to fix it. They recognize this and say, "Well, you know what, I'm so far I can't get over that hill." And now it just brings you to wherever the results of your actions bring you to and you say, "I give up."

However, it is never too late to bring your grade up. It is never too late to increase your numbers. For example, you may be 65, and your grade is low; your numbers are off. But you see a child who needs help. You do something to help that child change his trajectory, and he does something great in the world. Your numbers may increase dramatically from that one act.

Whatever your grade or numbers are, the report card helps you see what you have done so far, what you still need to do, and whether you have enough time to do it.

When this journey ends, the report card will determine where and what your next journey will be.

19

Dying Elders

Some elders feel anguish because they need to share their wisdom, but no one will listen to them. They are rejected, abandoned, and tossed away in homes for old people. Because they think that nobody cares, some get discouraged and want to die. When they die, the wisdom that could help future generations dies along with them.

An elder learned that he was facing his last days on earth; he was dying. His children and friends asked if they could come to see him. He said that he did not want to see anyone and had a letter written by his minister saying farewell. He asked that nobody contact him (although he did say they could contact his wife). Before that, he wanted to share his wisdom. However, in his last days, because he refused to see his family, he could not share what he was learning in his final moments with them.

If I were to say what selfishness looks like, the long handle-spoon metaphor is applicable. Selfishness looks like someone sitting with short arms and a long handle-spoon, trying to feed themself. They are trying to feed themself but cannot because the spoon is too long to reach their mouth. They can't get it to their mouth, but they keep trying to feed themself.

Being unselfish looks like the person having a long spoon, but he's feeding you. You have a long spoon, and you are feeding him. You are feeding each other with these spoons because you can reach each other and feed each other. I can feed you with my spoon. I'm not selfish. And now you are feeding me with your spoon. So we are both surviving, we're in the light, and we can thrive. But if I am selfish, I'm not going to eat; I will die and perish.

If selfish people try to feed themselves only, and the spoons are too long, they will perish by themselves. Those that live a life of caring and sharing, will feed each other. And they'll always be fed. They'll thrive and walk into the light together.

Messages to the True Descendants

This elder is acting selfishly. He is trying to feed himself with a long handle-spoon. And those around him who need to be fed by him because he's the elder are not being fed because he is not delivering. He is holding out; he is hoarding his wisdom. He is having his last final words and hoarding the information he's receiving in the night from the spirit world. He is supposed to be sharing with his family so they will be ready when their day comes. You are supposed to deliver the information if you can, not hold it.

In another case, an elder family member was on her deathbed and shared what she was experiencing. There was a call at two o'clock in the morning. She talked about the conversations that she was having with the spirit world. She was in that middle space between here and there. And she told me the things that it was telling her. She shared that with me to make sure I get it right before I get to that day.

She explained that you will face all that is left unresolved before the moment of crossing over. She shared the most painful memory of something she had done to another creature when she was young, living in Georgia in the 1930s.

One day she was hanging out some clothes and boiling some water for coffee. A black dog would hang around her because he loved her. But she found the dog to be annoying. Because the dog would not go away, she poured the boiling hot water on him. The dog hollered and hollered and eventually died. The sound of that screeching dog hurt her heart deeply. Because she felt so bad about what she had done, she vowed that she would do good from that day on.

She explained that she has to face that dog when she crosses over. Because she would cross paths with that dog, she had to apologize and ask for its forgiveness.

If you have done something that is not good, once you become aware, you must do everything in your power to do good from that day forward. You will never know when the day will come for you to cross over. When you do, you will face everything that you have done again. Because she was seeing and having experiences in the space between here and there, she said, "I am telling you this so you will know that you will face it again."

I understood and helped everybody understand what she was going through. When that day came, and she had to cross over, she was content. She was balanced because we had these conversations with each other. That's what family does; that's the bond. And family doesn't always mean your bloodline. It means that if I'm an elder, and this is someone I cherish, I should deliver the wisdom so that they can have a better day.

That's what the first elder is supposed to do. He's supposed to share the things he is learning close up and personal in the presence of spirit, the other world that he's on his way to, and the visits he is receiving to prepare him. He is supposed to pass it down to his family members. That's what elders do.

Elders are supposed to pass down to the generations, the generational stories. They are supposed to pass down stories about what it feels like and what it looks like when you are in the presence of godly spirits.

When they share their wisdom, you should listen.

20

Beyond the Light

We use our imagination to create stories and images of what we think is beyond the light, but you will never know. All over the world, it is said that God is unknowable.

If anybody claims they've seen what is beyond the light, they have not. You cannot because it is too powerful. You cannot even stare at a little light bulb, so imagine what would happen if you tried staring at that light. You will say "it's too much." Although you will never see what's beyond the light, you cannot deny that there is something behind it. And it is as powerful as can be.

When you travel the universe, come back to wherever your landing spot is, and remember what you experienced, you will recognize that it was an out-of-body experience. You were not in the flesh.

It is an out-of-body experience that allows you to transcend space and time. If you were to ever reach that high level of experience, you would never be able to say that you went beyond the light.

Now, when you are no longer earthbound, you can go beyond the light because you will become a part of it. However, you will never be able to be here in the flesh again. That's the final destination. You can never come back. If you go there, you will never be able to return to your physical body and describe what you experienced.

There is even a wall that prevents you from going beyond a certain level if you're not destined to be there. Say, for example, something happened, but it wasn't your time. You go there, but there is a wall. You get information, leave when your time ends there, and return to the flesh. You can talk about what it felt like to be in front of that wall. But you can never describe what it looked like behind the wall because if you go behind it, you are not coming back. It is a realm that is occupied by those who are not like us.

Messages to the True Descendants

Images have been created that claim to be the power beyond the light. They are an illusion and have been put in place to control you.

No one has been there, therefore no one can tell you what's beyond the light.

22

Spirit Mail

You have to go up and get your spirit mail. That is the reason people pray, it is why they meditate because they try to go high enough to get to their spirit mail, get the information, and bring it back down. Some get their spirit mail for themselves, while others get it to help others. I go up, get the mail, bring it back down, and give it to those who need it.

Spirit mail may not only come when you seek it. It can come through anything and anybody at any time. For example, the spirit world may need to deliver a message to you. First, it may try to talk to you. However, since many of us do not listen to our inner voice, it may try to reach us in a dream. However, many of us are disconnected from our dreams because we think they are not real.

We do not remember our dreams or know how to interpret them; thus, we may still not receive the message. Spirit may then try to reach out to someone around you or send a sign through some other means. But because we are not paying attention, because we are not listening, we miss the mail.

You may have a question and pray for answers. You ask, "God please tell me what to do about this or what to do about that?" You then wait for the answer. Then you say, "God did not hear me, my prayer was not answered." You say this while someone is right in front of you trying to give you the answer. They are trying to tell you what you need to know or are behaving in ways to show you, but you will not listen, and you do not see it because you expect the answer to fall from the sky.

It may be your child, your mother, father, spouse, friend, co-worker, whoever is around you or in your life. It may even be a stranger, but you will not listen because you do not know that spirit mail can come through anybody, you miss the mail and subsequently the answer you are seeking.

The world's religions teach us that a messenger, messiah, prophet, or deliverer is coming. They teach us that when humanity gets too off track when the spirit world wants to send a message, it seeks out or sends a messenger, a messiah, prophet, avatar, etc., to deliver what is needed to help humanity get back on track. This is the image in people's minds; in their memory, that judges what this should look like.

However, spirit mail comes to groups of people in different regions of the world depending on what they need at the time. It could be a small group or a large group, it could be in a particular community, local, or national. Those who get the spirit mail see what is needed in advance. That is what spirit mail is. You see it in advance. You see those who need it, and you deliver the message. It is not always as we imagine it to be.

Messengers, prophets, avatars, etc., are all around us. They come in different ways and bring spirit mail that delivers messages in different forms. They are all around us delivering messages of health and healing for ourselves and the planet. They are delivering messages of religious tolerance, racial harmony, gender equality, prosperity for all, peace, love, and unity. Spirit mail comes to us through the written word, spoken word, song, music, etc., and is expressed in all forms of media.

However, these messages are obscured by unhealthy messages of religious intolerance, racial disharmony, gender inequality, prosperity for a few, hate, war, and disunity.

There is always hope of a messiah, deliverer, messenger, avatar, etc., that will deliver a message that will reach all four corners of the earth. There is always hope that someone will deliver a message that will capture the hearts and minds of those in all four corners to create a vibration that will bring about change to the planet. Many have come, but their messages have never gotten to that high level of vibration thus far. But they have gotten to a vibration that is high enough that we keep on trying.

We will always keep trying because we know that it is possible. They have come, and hearts grew fonder. Hearts pounded and connected to a high level. They just have not gotten to the level of vibration needed to alter the rhythmic pattern of the vibration that was in motion at the time. And that is the case today. However, because it is a rhythmic pattern that we are working towards, we will be prepared when that moment arrives. It has to do with the configuration of the stars and planets that nothing we create on this planet can stop.

Until that time comes, continue to go up to get your spiritual mail and deliver it to those who need it. Just know that it comes in many ways and many forms. When you know that, there will be nothing that can block you from receiving it.

That is the power of spirit mail.

23

Meeting in the Garden

When we are children, we dream of a safe space we can go to when things are confusing, there is chaos around us, and we are afraid. We have that place in our mind we go to feel safe, peace, and harmony. My place happened to be a garden. It's a garden I saw and ascended to when I was a child. Then I got confirmation from ancient texts that showed that such a garden exists in the heavens. When I saw the garden in a book, I said, "Oh my God, that's where I've been going."

You went to a garden when you were a child. Would you explain that further?

When I was coming up, at around 16 or 17, I was getting messages about things from ancient times and places: the pyramids, ancient texts, ancient scriptures, ancient wall images, and ancient languages. Then I began receiving invitations from those who were a part of secret societies. I would be brought to places underground and taught to understand the messages that were coming to me. First, I would receive a message that people were coming. Then they would come. Some would just tell me things, others would take me underground for a month, six months, sometimes a year, or two or three years.

They would help me understand things I was privy to know in advance. As such, when I had certain experiences, I accepted them because I was told in advance that they were going to happen. I just didn't know when. So when moments came, I knew what and why. When they came, I knew. I saw the look. I saw the eyes. I saw the portals. I saw the location. The garden was one of them.

Are you saying the garden is a place?

It's a real location found in ancient texts that exist in other realms.

Messages to the True Descendants

Okay, you said people would come to you, tell you different things, and teach you. Then you said there was a garden. Would you explain that again?

A garden is a place I would ascend to and get information. Then I would come back and continue to live my life as a teenager going to school. I would get messages and very clear information about what to be aware of, and what to look to hear or see again.

I'd be walking, and suddenly, someone would approach me and say, "Hey, brother, I see that...." I'm not saying anything, they would just approach me. Then we'll be together for thirty days, sixty days, one, two, or three years in private underground settings going through ancient texts. And within that time frame, they'll cover all the things I was told to be aware of when I went to the garden.

Did you go to the garden before you started meeting these people? So you had an experience where you went to this place in your mind?

I ascended. It's not in my mind. I was outside of my body.

So you had an out-of-body experience?

Yes, which I found to be true and that's why I attached it to my reality. First, I have the experience, then see it in the physical world. I'll then meet someone to confirm it. Now, I know it's real.

Okay, so you will see something, or have a vision first. Then you have the experience in the physical world. Because you have the experience now you know it's real?

I accept what was revealed to me and continue the journey to understand it. Because the garden is my safe space, that's where I go to seek counsel whenever I need clarity.

I go there when I need to rest, be at peace, or have questions. Sometimes I have questions about experiences I am having that are very confusing. When I know what I'm experiencing is not based on my worthiness, I know it has to be something else. There must be some other purpose behind that moment. So when I get to that place, when I am completely exhausted and confused about what's going on in my life, I ascend to the garden. I ask, "What's the reason, what is it that I'm supposed to see? What am I supposed to learn as a result of all the misery, suffering, and sacrifice I have to go through in my life?" There are some situations and circumstances I can change at any time. Still, I maintain humility and keep my ego contained and choose to go through it and maintain trust and faith that what I'm experiencing has a greater purpose.

When I get to that place when I have had enough, and I need to be told what and why, I meet them in the garden, and we have a sit down like we are royalty. It's the most beautiful garden that you can imagine. I try to do my best by using my meager means to create that experience here. That's why I have a garden now. I try to replicate what I see there using the materials and the means I have here to create that same type of vibration.

That garden is a place that I ascend to regularly. That garden is a place of sanctity. That garden is where I go to seek counsel. When I go there, it's very clear. I go to that place, and I sit in the garden because that's the place I can be in peace and harmony. They sit beside me and then I ask them questions. Then they show and help me understand what I need to know.

So are you suggesting that we all have such a place?

Everyone has experiences and a place they can go to for answers. You have a safe space; a place you can go to for peace and harmony.

You just have to know that it is there, and it is real.

24

A Body in Motion

Life is a body in motion. A body has to be in motion because that's what it was created to be. We are always in motion creating, producing, and developing. How you deal with your thoughts and feelings makes your experiences difficult or easy.

Because a body has to always be in motion, that's what makes life. The day that your body is no longer in motion, you are going back to the earth. So, if you are a body in motion, and you have work to do, then all you have to say is, "I enjoy doing this work because I have the opportunity to be a body in motion." Whatever you must do, do it in peace, do it with respect, and do it with honor.

Many of us experience the pain of living in a world that is faced with many challenges.

However, regardless of the state of the world, or your situation or circumstances, you are still a body in motion. The reality in which you perceive your body in motion determines your experiences and how they affect you. A situation can be experienced as a burden or joy. You can let it cause you pain or pleasure.

You have no choice but to be a body in motion. It is up to you to make the best of it.

25

Under Your Feet

Some ideas are created to contaminate the truth. Many say that truth is based on one's perception of reality, but some truths are not. This truth is based on the reality that everything is connected. Although you are contained within yourself, within your own vibration, you are a part of everything.

> You are a part of the earth
> You are a part of the air
> You are part of the water
> You are part of the fire
> You are a part of the trees
> You are a part of the flowers
> You are a part of the sun, the moon and the stars

Messages to the True Descendants

> You are a part of all living creates that walk this planet
> You are a part of everything, and everything is a part of you.

Flocks of birds fly down after the rain. On top of the soil, there is no evidence of any subterranean creatures. However, they can feel them under their feet. They follow them; they put their beaks into the dirt and pull them out at the exact moment. They then fly back to the nest and feed their families. They know what is under the subterranean.

Like the birds, when you walk on the dirt, you can feel the subterranean creatures living in their communities. You can feel them under your feet. You must know about them to know who you are.

You must know these things. When you know these things, you will treat everything with love and compassion because you know you are a part of everything, and everything is a part of you.

Then you will be protected in all things and have nothing to worry about.

26

Man is Perfect

Everything in your life is masterfully created just for you. It is about what you need to become a better you so you can carry out your purpose.

We say that man is not perfect. What an insult it is to say to the Great Designer, the Great Orchestrator, the Great Conductor, the Omnipotent, the most profound reality that the mind of man works every day to try to comprehend where, why, and how this grand creation came to be, that something in it is flawed.

Do we think that the Great Designer does an incomplete job? Do we think that the Great Orchestrator would create something that is not perfect? We are told that we are not perfect, so get down on your knees and bow down to me. Who are we bowing to? If we say man is not perfect, then we are saying that The Great Designer is not perfect. We are bowing to something that is not perfect.

Are we saying that The Great Designer did not finish the job? If we are saying this, it means that everything is not in perfect order and will be finished at some point. If we are saying that the job is finished, then we accept that everything that we experience, made from earth, air, water, and fire, and all creatures that walk the planet, are in perfect harmony and perfect order. If we say that everything is in perfect order, how can we say that man, the greatest creation, is not perfect?

Saying that man is not perfect causes us to look elsewhere other than where we are to find perfection. Perfection lies inside you. Things are always changing, growing, and evolving to become better and greater. You are perfect in your evolvement and purpose. The Great designer will deliver to you what you need to evolve to become better and greater. This means that everything you experience, your character traits, and all, is about you growing and evolving.

When you know that and state it in the presence of others, you become accountable for becoming a better you. When you become a better you, you will become worthy of receiving the gifts you dream about. They will not come from UPS or US mail. They may knock at your door, but they are not the origin.

Everything is in perfect order. Man is perfect.

27

Spirit Data

Because everything is constantly changing and evolving, the I AM wants to accumulate data. Data is captured through minds that have evolved to where their experiences and the data being captured is evolved. It is captured through intelligence that is at a premium level based on its evolution. Even if the individual being used is not of the highest intelligence, but his faculties have evolved to a high level. His physical, mental, or spiritual capacity has evolved to where what is needed can be extracted. The person being used to capture data may not even be aware of it.

When data is being captured, there are active guardians to protect us and ensure that certain things don't come to pass and that what is needed is obtained. They are there to ensure that we do not encounter any mirrors or anything that shows a reflection because we are not supposed to see it.

Why are we not supposed to see it?

We are not supposed to see what happens when they come in. When the spirit comes in, there is a takeover of the body. Because of the vibration level on which they operate, they have the power to change your molecular structure. And that is where the mirrors come in.

If you saw yourself earlier, you would see the person you see every day. However, when a spirit comes in, you would see a different presence at that moment. It could be taller or smaller; it could be stronger. So, it changes the molecular structure when you are in the experience of that moment. If you look in the mirror, you will see that you are having an out-of-body experience; something else has taken over; its a takeover.

When you use the phrase, I AM, many may think you are referring to a particular religion or spiritual belief system. In using the I AM, are you putting what is infinite in a religious box?

If anybody understands the I AM, they know that the I AM is infinite. There is no box because the I AM is a part of everything. There are no walls in the I AM. Everything is a possibility. Everything is or is being, so everything is I AM. The I AM is in everything, even speech; the way we use our words and express our understanding is still part of the I AM.

What keeps anyone from receiving this understanding is only the barriers in their own mind. They must challenge their minds to break through and see the realm of possibilities because it is all about possibilities. Scientists, astrophysicists, quantum physicists, etc., are aware of this. If your mind can think it, it is possible. Whatever your mind can comprehend, imagine, or fathom, there is the possibility of it being real. The only limitation is your failure to understand that. Because everything is in the I AM, everything you think, feel, and experience is all possible because the I AM is in it all.

You speak of capturing intelligence at its highest level, what about intelligence at its lowest level, is there any value in capturing that?

The I AM captures intelligence from the highest and the lowest of a particular category. Because of the law of polarity, you must have the highest and the lowest. That's how you find where the balance is. Since everything is about balance, you must have the highest and the lowest.

Even with humanity, we must look at the difficulties that the lower mind experiences, sees, feels, or whatever it goes through, as well as understand the highest mind and how it sees, feel or go through things to understand where the middle is. When we fail to do this, it leads to a disconnect and the whole point is to try to bridge it together.

Okay. You said that the I AM wants to capture the highest and lowest intelligence. You said that there is a takeover and that spirits capture the data. So, is God capturing data or are other entities doing it?

There are many essences of God. The essences of God exist on many different levels. At every level, there is an arm. There is the top and then there are realms that have commanders who are under them. For simplicity's sake, if I had ten major supreme vibrations, they may vibrate in different realms. The elements; earth, air, fire, and water, take commands from them. Earth, air, water, and fire are all equal where they exist. However, they are not at the top. They are only levels from the top.

People have been given a concept that there is only God Almighty. However, many spiritual forces and entities exist, and many roam this planet. As many people as there are, there are that many spirits. And the spirits have different levels that control them. That is difficult for the mind of man to receive. There are other worlds right beside our own that are beyond the vision of our eyes. And they are very active. We just can't see them, but they are there. So yes, there are many.

If the I AM commands to receive information from a certain area or category, it will send entities to get it. They see through my body; through my eyes to you. It's just an extension that spreads through it all. In the creation, there are no disconnected lines. None. That is how the I AM can see all because it has extensions to all through many ways.

If the I AM already knows everything, why would it need to capture data?

The I AM is a part of your changing experiences, and the I AM is changing with you.

28

The Balance

They will unleash the smallest, most microscopic, most powerful enemy against you. You'll never see it, and it can kill you before you know it's there. It is just a warning to let you know that they are here. It's your choice. Either you listen, or you die. How do you die? It will cut off your oxygen, and you can't breathe. You cannot live without air.

Some of us know that the world is going back to balance. You know this, and you can see it. However, you don't know when or how it is going to happen. You just know that things have to balance, and it's going to happen.

So you keep seeing things. You see occurrences, incidents, events, the future, but you don't know when it's going to happen. You keep looking for it. Before you know it, years have gone by. You are now old and gray and have gone mad wondering whether what you thought you knew was real or not. Then it happens.

What keeps you from going insane amid all the chaos occurring now and that to come, is nature. Nature can bring you back to balance.

The hummingbirds bring you back.

The flowers and the trees bring you back.

The fresh air brings you back.

The moon that lights up the night sky that looks down on you and tells you that you are in the right place at the right time brings you back.

Then the sun comes up again. And you see all the curvatures of the universe and the rays of color in the morning dew.

29

Do You and Let Me Do Me

I have the power to open the gates. Nothing has anything on me. I send my powers, and they do my work. I come for those who are true down to their soul because that is where I hear; that is where I lie. When I have delivered all the tests to you, including pain and sorrow, and you never waver, I know that you hear me. Now I will set you free. Just do you and let me do me.

> Doing you may just be being a good mother or father for your children.
> Doing you may be doing well in school so you can become a great scientist.

Messages to the True Descendants

> Doing you may be being a great storyteller to give hope and encouragement for those coming behind you.
>
> Doing you may be being a builder so that you can create and construct.
>
> Doing you may be learning biology so that when the fish in the sea are sick, you will know how to bring them back to balance and know what to do for the suffering corals.

I have the power to deliver an elixir, where one drop can free all from pain and suffering because I am the master of all masters of the elixirs.

No one knows where they are because they are in all corners of the earth. I will deliver them to those who are worthy so that they can give them to those who need to be free of pain and suffering.

I am the master of all masters of all elixirs. Do you and let me do me.

30

Diamond Doorways

What makes the diamond the greatest and most powerful gemstone on the planet is all the curvatures, and the many things you can see when looking through one.

If you look through a diamond with a scope, you see many doors. You see different colors, auras, realms of time, and dimensions. You can see all of these things through a diamond. That's why the greatest, most powerful diamonds were taken out of the hands of man and put in museums. It is so that you cannot see these things.

Those who hold the diamonds hold the wealth. It is not just the value placed on them that gives those who possess them, their wealth. They showed them where the wealth was. They then used this knowledge to strip the earth of the

Messages to the True Descendants

elements containing the vibrations needed to produce what people need to survive and thrive.

All one has to do is put the largest, most powerful diamond that exists[1] on a mount and let the sun shine through in a certain position at a location, and you will see the doorways to everything, you will see the doorways to it all.

If you mount the diamond in front of certain pillars, archways, waterways, on certain mountains, or at a certain location in the ocean, and let the sun shine through, you can see all the curvatures of time and space, and many magical things.

You can see the ages, the past, and the future.

You can see mystical cities, ancient and future ones.

You can see royalty; future queens, and kings. You can see all those mystical creatures, locations, and cities passed down through folklore that are now replicated and sold to us through entertainment as if they are not real.

---

[1] The largest known diamond found to date is the Cullinan, 530-carat diamond. It was originally 3,106 carats before being cut into nine pieces. It is in the British royal collection

You can see all those things right through that space.

You can see doorways to everything, with your very own eyes; you can see right into heaven.

You can even see you.

31

Unified Heartbeats

How do we get the attention of the elements?

How do we get air's attention?
How do we get water's attention?
How do we get fire's attention?
How do we get the earth's attention?

The true descendants knew how.

When you see a parade, and everybody is in sequence, it creates a sphere that seems to be an impenetrable force because everybody is on one accord.

When you see an army with everyone marching together, it creates a sphere and appears to be an impenetrable force because everyone is on one accord.

The world was designed for things to be in rhythm and exact sequence; the seasons, the growth of trees and plants, blooming of the flowers; it is all in rhythm and sequence.

It is the same with the heartbeat. There is a certain vibration that comes through the heart that goes from heart to heart. When your heart beats, it comes out of your body and puts ripples in the air, and catches the next person's heartbeat. If the hearts are on one accord, they will become unified, and you cannot penetrate them; they create a sphere.

The power of many on one accord can get what is needed because it can communicate with the elements using words and tones and then spin them far, wide, and expansive enough because of the vibration of the ripple effect of unified heartbeats.

The heartbeats among many with the tone of the chant light the fire that pushes them up to where the power of all powers lies. Because it is so pure, it delivers what they are requesting.

Unified heartbeats on one accord have the power to do this and can change the direction of humanity and the planet.

If we can get all the heartbeats beating in the right way in the right direction with the right understanding, they can become one heartbeat because they are in the same rhythm. They are in sequence.

If we can synch our heartbeats so that they become unified, we can cover every corner of this planet with vibrations of peace, love, acceptance, harmony, and balance. With that, we can change the world.

32

Stacking Signs

You have to know how they stack the signs and how they line them up. For example, he kept showing me all the crop dusting, all the signs and symbols that they were leaving from the beginning of the evolution of humanity to give the illusion of the possibility that it might not be other entities creating them, that man may have created them. So, there's always an out game. The imagination will go both ways. Man will think either he created these things or something else did. It will remain a mystery. They will convince themselves of this, so their work is very easily done. Man will dupe himself.

He said this is how we do it. Since man has grown to even question these things, since the beginning of time, we started leaving signs and symbols on grassy lands and in locations throughout the world. We make sure that man will see them before they disappear. It doesn't matter what the climate is; whether it is hot or cold, wet or dry, they will be there long enough so that someone can see them before they disintegrate.

We have been stacking signs and symbols for a very long time. But man has been finding them off sequence. They may have found one in the 19th century that we left 10,000 BC. They don't know, they're trying to figure out the time they were placed using graph time, but they don't know. They don't know that we stack them. So if you stack them from the first one to the last one, this is the key that will unlock the door to what we are trying to convey.

We see the signs and symbols but are not able to interpret them. We are not able to understand them because of where we are in our evolution. There is a communication gap because they are communicating in their language. It is just like if Voyagers 1 or 2 with the Gold Record containing various types of media launched in 1977 were to land on a planet or somewhere in space and its inhabitants found it. Because their way of communicating may be vastly different from ours, they would not understand what we are trying to convey.

It is the same thing with the signs and symbols that are found all over the world. Many of the markings and structures are signs and symbols in a language that we don't understand. In terms of our evolution, we are like Neanderthals. They can only leave signs and symbols in the language of the space and time dimensions that they exist in. They are trying to tell us the origins, source, location, and what is next in their language. The key to unlocking the signs is stacking them in the chronological order in which they were left. When we can do that, the message will be clear.

If something needs to communicate with us, why would it just not be able to do so?

The ability to communicate with us was cut off. There is something else on the planet, an invader; an intruder that has infiltrated the planet and has been causing all the chaos. So the communication has been blocked. Because it has been blocked, we have been blocked. So because of the infiltrator, we got disconnected. We don't understand the signs because we got disconnected. They had to block it. They had to block them because if some things are communicated, it will lead to disaster.

The problem with the prophets that have come to the planet is that they come in their time, in their region of the planet, speaking their language. Therefore, only those in their region of the world received the message. They, therefore, have never been able to deliver the message that was pure from the source to every corner of the planet before it was blocked or snubbed.

With artificial intelligence (AI), there is the potential for the message to be translated worldwide, in different languages simultaneously so that those all over the world can receive it. There is the potential for the messages to be received worldwide before the intruder can intercept them. Because, through machine learning, it will do it by itself.

If someone wants to read what is written in English, it will come directly in their language just using the computer. AI is the only source that gives us the capacity to change the text to every language on the planet at the same time. Man can't do it. He doesn't have the capacity. Only AI does because information from every corner of the planet has been entered into the database. Prophets or deliverers were not capable of doing that. Only AI is. For example, I can ask my phone, "Tell me what this says in the Yugoslavian language?"

We are just getting to a place where we can understand what some of the signs and symbols are trying to tell us. You could not do that in the 1960s, the 1990s, or even ten years ago. Only now, in 2021 with AI, do we have the capacity to understand what they are trying to tell us and can communicate it in different languages all over the world.

Man is always going to search for answers. Scientific communities will continue to try to figure these things out. This they know. Man has been trying to get these answers the moment that they recognized that another entity existed. Since they have existed, man has been trying to find them and figure them out. They have been trying to figure out how they communicate; their language.

Man has been trying to figure out how everything on this planet listens to source, follows instructions, and why he doesn't. The birds do what they do because the birds follow the instructions from source. The leaves fall off the trees and grow back because they follow instructions from source. The seasons change; summer, spring, fall, and winter come and go because they follow the instructions from source. We are the only ones that do not. The reason for this is that we have been infiltrated. Some cultures still follow the voice and instructions from source. Those societies that are integrated with modern technology are the ones that are interfered with the most. They are the ones that have been the most cut off from following instructions from source.

But man has been wayward for a very long time, way before industry and modern technology.

Man was not meant to be at war and kill each other and do all those kinds of things. Man wasn't designed for that. He was designed to keep the harmony, but we got invaded. Because of the rays of light that they use, we don't recognize how they look. If you were to recognize them, then you'd ask, why would I take orders or follow this? If this looks like that? It's not a derivative of man. It's a created derivative of man as best as they could do to look like us so they could fit in. That's the best they could do, but they're missing a key element. There is an element that they don't have.

They don't have the cell. They do not have the cell in the back of their mind that can be called and told what to do. They are not capable of listening and hearing. If you listen to source, you will not have to worry about the false power, with false images and expectations driving humanity insane because you will see behind it.

All source has to do is let you know that the vibration and movement of the planet are about to change so that the sun will shine differently. When the sun shines differently, it's going to shine through in a way that you will see all the dimensions, doorways, entities, and all the presences that man is in company with on this planet. You will not have to worry because you will be protected.

What is the goal? For what reason do they need to communicate with us?

This message is the beginning of a process. For those who have lost the connection, the aim is for this message to vibrate in your hearts and minds and to open the communication channel between you and spirit.

Is this because they are trying to get to the right people, without communicating with the intruders?

Everyone has to be notified before the intruders can snub the message, preventing them from catching it. That's what they've been doing from the beginning of time. It's like a man on a horse trying to warn the people, but he is shot down in the forest. So he never gets the message to the people.

What's their goal? Why would something intrude on this planet? What do they have to gain?

They want to gain the power to control the planet so that they can enjoy all the beauty that this planet has to offer. When you experience this, that God made so beautiful, you don't want to leave it because no other place has been created like this. No location in any other universe has the beauty of this planet.

Messages to the True Descendants

It is not until now that man has created a mechanism that can do what only AI can do. Because there are so many different languages, only AI can deliver a message to all corners of the earth in all languages before its transmission is blocked.

What is it that they are trying to communicate with us? What do they want us to know?

When the time comes, they will speak to you in a clear voice in the language that you understand. Those who have been awakened; those who are listening; those who are the true descendants will hear them, and they will tell you what they want you to know, and you will know what to do.

www.ingramcontent.com/pod-product-compliance
Lightning Source LLC
LaVergne TN
LVHW091553060526
838200LV00036B/813